# About This Resource

## Why is this topic important?

Businesses and organizations are being challenged to encourage the spirit of innovation in order to maintain a creative edge in the global marketplace. We've all had years of schooling in how to think logically, but it is just as important, if not more so, to think creatively. This resource can be used to help teach people at all levels of the organization to work together in building powerful collaborative relationships. It is not only possible, but essential, to train people to think more creatively. It will bring more energy and excitement to the workplace and increase individual and group productivity.

## What can you achieve with this resource?

This Facilitator's Guide is designed to help learners explore what creativity is, how it can be learned and enhanced, and how to explore and overcome the barriers to creative thinking. Learners will learn how to manage their creative talents and maximize vitality in the workplace. Learners will also discover how to make career choices that enrich their jobs by utilizing their creative strengths. Once learners discover where their strengths lie, they can determine who the best people are for them to collaborate with and can build powerful relationships. Teams that recognize and use the creative strengths of all individual members become more productive.

## How is this resource organized?

This resource consists of two pieces: this Facilitator's Guide and a separate *Creative Style Profile*. *The Facilitator's Guide* provides step-by-step instructions for leading a workshop based on the *Creative Style Profile*. It includes suggested scripts, individual and group exercises and activities, and supporting training materials, including overhead, handout, and flip-chart masters. The Creative Style Profile includes an introduction to creativity, the profile itself, and scoring and interpretation information.

# About Pfeiffer

Pfeiffer serves the professional development and hands-on resource needs of training and human resource practitioners and gives them products to do their jobs better. We deliver proven ideas and solutions from experts in HR development and HR management, and we offer effective and customizable tools to improve workplace performance. From novice to seasoned professional, Pfeiffer is the source you can trust to make yourself and your organization more successful.

**Essential Knowledge** Pfeiffer produces insightful, practical, and comprehensive materials on topics that matter the most to training and HR professionals. Our Essential Knowledge resources translate the expertise of seasoned professionals into practical, how-to guidance on critical workplace issues and problems. These resources are supported by case studies, worksheets, and job aids and are frequently supplemented with CD-ROMs, websites, and other means of making the content easier to read, understand, and use.

**Essential Tools** Pfeiffer's Essential Tools resources save time and expense by offering proven, ready-to-use materials—including exercises, activities, games, instruments, and assessments—for use during a training or team-learning event. These resources are frequently offered in looseleaf or CD-ROM format to facilitate copying and customization of the material.

Pfeiffer also recognizes the remarkable power of new technologies in expanding the reach and effectiveness of training. While e-hype has often created whiz-bang solutions in search of a problem, we are dedicated to bringing convenience and enhancements to proven training solutions. All our e-tools comply with rigorous functionality standards. The most appropriate technology wrapped around essential content yields the perfect solution for today's on-the-go trainers and human resource professionals.

**Pfeiffer**
www.pfeiffer.com   *Essential resources for training and HR professionals*

Pfeiffer™

# Diversity Awareness Profile (DAP)

## Facilitator's Guide

*Second Edition*

Karen M. Stinson

BICENTENNIAL
1807
WILEY
2007
BICENTENNIAL

John Wiley & Sons, Inc.

ISBN: ISBN: 978-0-7879-9554-6

Acquiring Editor: Lisa Shannon
Director of Development: Kathleen Dolan Davies
Developmental Editor: Susan Rachmeler
Production Editor: Dawn Kilgore
Editor: Rebecca Taff
Manufacturing Supervisor: Becky Carreño
Design, composition, technical art: Leigh McLellan Design

Printed in the United States of America
Printing

# Contents

# Acknowledgments

· · · · · · · · · · · · · · · · · · ·

IN THIS GUIDE to the *Diversity Awareness Profile,* my goal has been to help you make your use of it a positive experience for you and your participants—one that is as insightful and informative as possible. I have tried to distill what I have learned over the last twenty years as a pioneer in the diversity field. During that time, I have learned from many family members, friends, clients, colleagues, and total strangers who wanted to help with our mission. I am grateful to all of them. I want to especially acknowledge:

- The brilliant staff of ProGroup, who are always willing to be our "living lab." Their advice on the revisions of the DAP was invaluable.

- Aimee Linkewich, who managed this project and worked closely with me to create the new, revised DAP and facilitator's guide.

- Myrna Marofsky, my business partner and best friend, who partners with me in the ongoing creative search for new and better ways to help clients.

- My daughter, Darcy Grote, who joined me in my work ten years ago and brings me hope for the next generation with her insights and leadership in the field. The next revision of the DAP will be on her capable shoulders.

# A Note from the Author

●●●●●●●●●●●●●●●●●●●●●●●

I STARTED PROGROUP, INC., twenty years ago with a clear vision—"To create a better world"—and a mission that hasn't changed in twenty years. Our mission has always been: "To work in partnership with organizations to create workplaces where everyone feels valued and respected and all employees have the opportunity to perform to their full potential."

As a woman who had worked in many male-dominated organizations, I knew what it felt to be a "diverse individual" who wasn't always listened to or offered the same opportunities as the men. In fact, I had decided to start my own company so that I could work toward my personal vision and mission without anyone telling me I wasn't appropriate or capable or qualified or ready.

However, I knew that I only had one perspective—that of a woman. I wanted to know the stories and experiences of others who were minorities or different from the norm in their organizations and what got in their way or blocked their success. I wanted to know what little or big things caused them to give up and stay or get up and leave. To find out, I used my network and invited groups of people to come to our offices and talk about their experiences in corporate America. Over a series of weeks, my team and I talked to groups of African Americans, Asian Americans, Latinos, Latinas, people with disabilities, older employees, young employees, women, people with HIV and AIDS, large people, and other groups I can't even remember anymore. We asked them to tell us what their work experiences were like for them. We asked them what behaviors by others in their organizations helped them succeed and perform to their full potential and what behaviors by others made it hard for them to contribute and use their skills and talents. We used this data to create the foundations of ProGroup's educational models and training programs, including the first version of the *Diversity Awareness Profile*.

The *Diversity Awareness Profile* was created as a tool to be given to participants during training sessions so that they could do an honest personal assessment of their attitudes and behaviors toward others who are different from them. We linked the scoring to a model I created called The Awareness Spectrum™ so that participants' scores on the instrument would link directly to a model that told them what their scores meant in terms of their everyday actions and behaviors at work. I thought that made the DAP much more practical because, based on their scoring, they could take actions to change their behaviors, which would improve their performance. The DAP is a useful aid and popular tool that thousands of individuals have taken in the last twenty years as a part of their personal development and awareness.

Since 2006 is the twentieth anniversary of the *Diversity Awareness Profile,* we decided it was time to review the instrument to make sure it is still relevant today. To do so, we once again held many focus groups and interviews of diverse individuals and asked them the same questions. This updated and revised DAP is the result. I hope it provides your employees and seminar participants with some useful personal insights that they will utilize to do their part in creating more respectful cultures in their workplaces.

Karen Stinson
January 2007

# Before You Start

## History of the DAP

The DAP was created by Karen Stinson, the founder and CEO of ProGroup, one of the top diversity consulting firms in the country. Karen started ProGroup in 1986 when diversity wasn't considered an issue in corporate America. However, in her work with many organizations, she noticed that the demographics were changing and that people didn't know how to handle the increased diversity, let alone leverage it to make their organizations stronger. Karen thought it would be helpful to have a self-assessment that provided individuals with an opportunity to reflect on their behaviors in the workplace. No such instrument existed, as Karen was a pioneer in the field of diversity, so she and her team decided to create one.

Karen and her team conducted dozens of focus groups and one-on-one interviews with people who had experience being minorities in their organizations. They targeted women, African Americans, Asian, Latinos and Latinas, immigrants, people with accents or English as a second language, people of all religions, large people, small people, married people, single people, divorced people, introverts, extroverts, and every other difference that might make a difference in organizations.

The first version of the DAP was created twenty years ago when diversity in the workplace was starting to build. Over time, it has been revised and updated based on follow-up focus groups, interviews, and data gathered in thousands of seminars to ensure that it encompasses current diversity issues and differences that make a difference in *today's* workplace.

## Applications

### Pre-Training

The *Diversity Awareness Profile* (DAP) can be utilized prior to a training session or workshop as a tool for participants to reflect on their behaviors in the work environment and discern where they fit within the Awareness Spectrum™. The DAP introduces the concept of diversity and provides language that can help participants think about it and talk about it before and during the session.

### During Training

The assessment can be incorporated as a component of many training programs, such as orientation, communication, assertiveness, management skills, or team building, to introduce language around diversity and show application of covered concepts in the participants' current behavior. The DAP can be used as a starting point to build learning and understanding around diversity and inclusion and to allow participants to see possible areas for improvement. This learning can be a key piece of any program in which the objectives involve working with today's increasingly diverse workforce or marketplace.

### Follow-Up/Post-Training

We recommend that participants take the DAP again six months later to assess where they are on the Awareness Spectrum™ now that they have completed the training and are incorporating the learning points into their work environments. Taking the DAP as a follow-up to a training reinforces the connection between behaviors and actions and their impact in the workplace.

### Refresher

The DAP assessment can be used as a tool to refresh the concepts discussed in a diversity training session or workshop. Taking the DAP at a later time allows the individuals to reflect on their behavior and utilize their learnings from the session. It also helps participants see their progress and identify areas for which they may need some coaching.

### Coaching

The DAP can also be used as a coaching tool when incorporating diversity competence into an employee's development. By taking the DAP, individuals can ascertain where they are on the Diversity Awareness Spectrum™ and create their own action plans accordingly. The manager/coach can use the suggestions listed in this guide for ways to improve and discuss specifics that are relevant to that person's work environment and performance challenges.

## Recommendation

We recommend that, when the DAP is part of an educational program, it be placed on the agenda after you have spent some time with individuals or class participants laying some groundwork. It seems to fit well after the awareness segment and before the skills application part. Participants get more out of the DAP when some time has been spent on the following:

- ▨ Definitions
    - ☐ What diversity and inclusion are
- ▨ Your organization's business case for diversity
    - ☐ Why creating an inclusive and respectful environment is important to your organization
- ▨ Awareness
    - ☐ How our biases and preferences, both positive and negative, can affect our behaviors
    - ☐ Organizational expectations of everyone to act respectfully toward others

If you administer the DAP at this point, people are more open to looking at their own behaviors. We recommend that you then follow it with a skill model to become an effective change agent and a segment during which the participants practice the skill model with customized case studies or scenarios. After that, they can complete action plans about what they will do individually to create and sustain a respectful and inclusive culture in your workplace.

# Preparing to Administer the DAP

## Materials Needed

- A copy of the DAP for each individual

- Pens or pencils for participants

- PowerPoint® slides (optional; see PowerPoint® Text section of this guide; a presentation of these slides is available online at www.pfeiffer.com/go/dap)

## Overview of the Facilitator's Guide

This guide was put together to help facilitators successfully administer the DAP as a part of a diversity education curriculum. It walks the facilitator through the preparation, administration, and debriefing of the DAP. We recommend that facilitators read through the entire guide prior to each time they administer the assessment. Doing so will remind the facilitator of all of the learning points and maximize the impact of the DAP on each participant.

# Purpose of the DAP

TELL THE PARTICIPANTS, "The purpose of taking the *Diversity Awareness Profile* is to give each of you an opportunity to privately evaluate your behaviors toward your colleagues and customers in your day-to-day interactions at work. The more honest you are as you complete the instrument, the more awareness you will gain about your own behaviors and the possible impact of those behaviors on others in your organization, especially those who are different from you."

Display the Objectives overhead and review the objectives with the participants.

# Administering the DAP

TELL PARTICIPANTS, "The DAP is just an educational tool to increase self-awareness. It has not been statistically validated. The results will not go into your employment records or to your manager. You will not be asked to hand it in after class. It is yours to use for your own development. So relax and get as much as you can out of this experience."

*Note to Facilitator:* Make sure you have discussed the usage of the DAP with your client prior to making the above statement and that the client agrees to use the DAP as you stipulate.

Give a copy of the DAP and a pen or pencil to each participant. Next, say to participants, "Now, please read the first page of the DAP. Look at the graphic carefully. Think of all of the dimensions of diversity that are present in your workplace and all of the ways that people are different from you. As you complete the DAP, keep all of the dimensions of diversity shown on page 1 of the assessment in your mind."

Display the Instructions overhead and read the following instructions out loud:

1. Read each statement and circle the number that best fits your behavior.

2. Remember that there are no right or wrong answers.

3. Be as honest and candid as possible with your responses.

4. Consider each statement in terms of your personal values, beliefs, actions and reactions, and experiences.

5. When you are finished, total the numbers you circled and write that total at the bottom of the page.

Say, "Don't second-guess your answers. If you answer each question honestly, it's the right answer for you. As you take the DAP, think about how you act on a typical day, not a day when you are in a really bad mood or a day when you are perfect and angelic, but just a typical day."

Tell the participants that they will be given up to 15 minutes to take the DAP. If they finish before the others, they can score their DAPs and read what their scores mean, but they are not to go to the action planning phase on the last page and should please remain quiet until others finish. Ask participants not to talk to you or others about their scores until everyone has finished.

# Debriefing

●●●●●●●●●●●●

ONCE EVERYONE has completed the DAP, it is time to introduce the Diversity Awareness Spectrum™. Display the Diversity Awareness Spectrum and tell the participants that you are going to talk them through it and give them some insight into what their results mean if, based on their scoring, they ended up as Naïve, Perpetuators, Avoiders, Change Agents, or Fighters.

Display the Debriefing overhead and leave it up while you describe each category.

## ◼ Naïve

Say, "I will start with Naïve. You'll note in the Spectrum that the Naïve category doesn't have a score. Not many people end up in this category. Naïve people are so clueless about their biased words and actions that they don't actually get a true score. So even if there is a Naïve person in this room, the rest of you would be much more likely to be aware of it than he or she would.

"Naïve people go around making offensive, inappropriate statements to or about people. Even scarier, they are likely making decisions or taking actions based on their naïve beliefs, which are probably illegal and certainly aren't in alignment with company policies and guidelines concerning discrimination. They have a narrow view of the world and have made little effort to find out what it's like to be someone other than themselves.

"For example, a Naïve manager may not be promoting females or offering them opportunities because of what that manager believes to be the 'truth' about women. An example would be, 'I won't promote her because then she would have to travel and she can't because she has children.' Naïve co-workers may tell or laugh at inappropriate jokes without realizing they are reinforcing negative stereotypes. They may be heard using derogatory terms for certain cultural groups without realizing that they are insulting people because they haven't thought about where those terms come from or what they mean.

"If you scored naïve or, more accurately, you determine from this description that you may be naïve, my advice to you is to start learning about others today! Make an effort with your team and colleagues to find out what you are saying and doing that is offending your co-workers and clients. Once you find out, thank them for the input and stop saying and doing those things.

"Next, identify people and organizations that could be your educators and cultural guides. They can be people within your team, your company, or your community who have different life experiences and perspectives than you. The differences between you can be gender, age, race, background, job, size, religion, sexual orientation, language, or many others. Start with the differences that you believe you should be developing more awareness and acceptance of. Spend time with your guides. When they talk, listen and learn. Thank them for the valuable lessons.

"Don't stop with individuals. Find out other sources for your education. Read about other cultures, go to movies that are created in other countries, attend festivals and events that celebrate other cultures, broaden your horizons and perspectives.

"Doing all of this doesn't mean you won't continue to make mistakes or offend people. No one is perfect, and we may at times unknowingly offend someone. However, as you work on it, you will offend people less often and people will be more understanding because they know you are honestly trying. I guarantee that making this effort will enrich your life, make you more successful at work, and make you a better member of your community.

"As you commit to learning and start this journey, realize that it will change you forever because you can only be naïve once. Once you know the impact of your words and actions, you either have to commit to and start the journey to being a change agent or continue those behaviors knowing the impact of them. That puts you in the Perpetuator category, which is the next category on the Diversity Awareness Spectrum™."

## Perpetuator (24 through 47)

"If you scored in the Perpetuator range, beware. This score means that you are purposefully saying and doing things that perpetuate negative stereotypes. Unlike Naïve people, who are clueless about the impact of their misconceptions, you know that your sexist, racist, ageist, or other biased words and actions are inappropriate and are causing harm to others, personally and professionally, but you do it anyway. Sometimes Perpetuators act this way because it gets them attention or power. Sometimes they act this way because they feel bonded with other Perpetuators and they think there's comfort in numbers.

"Whatever your reason, my advice to you is to *stop*! Your perpetuating behavior is a danger to your company and puts your own employment at risk.

"If you realize that you want to change, the first step is to admit what you've been doing and to stop it. You may want to spend some time thinking about why you have been acting or reacting in a negative way toward certain groups of people. Based on that, you may need some coaching or education. It might help you to get together with members of groups you have difficulty with and have some honest dialogue on how to build your knowledge and understanding of their history and what they bring to the workplace and community.

"The next step is to acknowledge to others you work with that you have been acting inappropriately. I recommend that you apologize to the people at work who have been negatively impacted by your comments or behaviors and tell them that you are making a real commitment to speaking and acting in a more respectful way. Ask them to have patience with you and to help you by calling you on inappropriate remarks or Perpetuator behavior. When they do what you asked, don't get mad or ridicule them. Thank them.

"As you go about your job, be more aware of when your biases and assumptions are influencing your behaviors and decisions so you can set them aside and act with respect toward everyone.

"As a result, you will be more respected by the professionals you work with and you will be more valuable to your organization. There is a downside. The Perpetuators you used to hang out with will be upset with you. They may call you names and say that you 'sold out' or are 'wimpy' or a 'brown-noser' or worse. Remember, reaction is their problem, not yours. You can try to invite them along into the 21st century and educate them, but it may not work."

## Avoider (48 through 71)

"Most people who take the DAP score as Avoiders. If you fall into this category, it means that you work at being respectful of others and don't normally perpetuate stereotypes or act inappropriately. However, people in this category tend to avoid conflict and do little or nothing when they witness others acting disrespectfully. By doing or saying nothing, you are assumed to be a 'silent supporter' by those who witness your reaction to the comments and actions of naïve or perpetuating people, or by the Perpetuators themselves. Even if you are rationalizing your Avoider behavior with statements such as, 'Everyone is entitled to an opinion,' or 'That's just the way she is,' or 'He doesn't mean anything by it and he's retiring soon anyhow,' or 'She's just blowing off steam,' recognize that your decision to do nothing is detrimental to creating and maintaining a respectful environment in your workplace.

"I believe that you want to work in a respectful, inclusive environment. If I am right, then you have a responsibility to do your part to create and maintain a positive environment for everyone. If you are a manager or supervisor, you have no choice but to speak up and address negative behaviors. An integral part of your job is creating and maintaining an environment in which everyone feels valued, everyone is treated respectfully, and everyone has a chance to perform to his or her full potential. If you are a manager, you can't be an Avoider and do your job well; you have to be a Change Agent.

"If you have been in the habit of being an Avoider, speaking out takes a lot of practice and courage. If you don't know what to say or how to say it, find someone who is used to being a Change Agent and ask that person to help you prepare and practice for dealing with a colleague who is Naïve, a Perpetuator, or a Fighter. Then have the courageous conversation. Once it's over, meet with your coach and debrief the discussion. Celebrate the conversations that go well and figure out another approach for the ones that go poorly. You will learn and develop skills as a Change Agent that translate to being a stronger, more valuable employee to both your team and your organization."

## Change Agent (72 through 83)

"If your score is in the Change Agent range, congratulations! You speak up when you hear inappropriate comments. You say something when you notice others making decisions or taking action based on biases or assumptions. Being a Change Agent isn't always comfortable or rewarding for you, but you feel that you don't have a choice. You have to act when you are aware that others are operating from somewhere else on the Diversity Awareness Spectrum™ and that it is causing damage to others, your culture, or your organization.

"Effective Change Agents speak to people about inappropriate behaviors or actions in a clear, professional, nonjudgmental manner. As a Change Agent, you approach people respectfully, with an understanding of where they are on the Diversity Awareness Spectrum™ and knowing what you want to achieve in the conversation. If they are Naïve, your first goal will be to educate them. If they are Perpetuators, you want to first stop them and then try to educate or enlighten them. If they are Avoiders, encourage and coach them to help them develop Change Agent skills. If they are Change Agents, support them. If they are Fighters, commend their passion and positive intent, but educate them about the negative impact of their approach and coach them on how to improve it. Recommend another way of acting that will help Fighters achieve their goals.

"If you are lucky enough to have other Change Agents on your team, seek out coaching and support from each other when needed. Support is very helpful, as Change Agents' comments are often not received with open ears. Efforts to do the right thing can blow up in your face. When that happens, it's invaluable to be able to go to another Change Agent and say, 'I approached the person this way and he reacted this way. It didn't work. Now what?' Help and support one another.

"Remember that creating and sustaining a culture of respect is achievable with enough Change Agents. Without them, it's impossible."

# Fighter (84 through 96)

"If your score is in the Fighter range, the good news is that you care about creating a respectful environment for everyone, especially people who are historically discriminated against. The bad news for you, and for your organization, is that your method is getting in the way of achieving your goals.

"Too often, Fighters feel so strongly about stopping injustice and are so vigilant about spotting bias and prejudice that they attack and judge, rather than educate or enlighten. Although pouncing on people may give you a temporary sense of satisfaction, you have probably learned from your experiences that it doesn't lead to the results you are seeking. You have probably noticed that very seldom does someone you verbally attack say, 'You know, you're right, and I feel motivated to make you happy and give you satisfaction by doing what you say.' The normal reaction to being attacked is to defend, deny, get even, or get away as quickly as possible. Their ongoing reaction is to start avoiding you.

"My advice to you Fighters is to think about your goal of respect and inclusion for everyone and make a commitment to modeling that goal in how you approach others that you see as Perpetuators or Naïve. If you need coaching and feedback, ask a Change Agent you know to help you modify your style. Keep the passion for fairness and equality and develop the best skills you can to make it happen in your workplace. You'll know it's working when people stop flinching or heading in the other direction when they see you coming."

# Questions and Answers

Ask participants for any comments or clarifying questions. Use the above information to respond. If you get questions you cannot answer, email them to kmstinson @progroupinc.com and you will get a reply.

*Note to Facilitator:* We recommend that you let participants keep their scores as confidential as they want to. Do not ask for a show of hands for each category. Do not have participants move around to sit with people with similar scores. Tell them that whatever score they ended up with is a result of their own rankings and that it is what it is. Remind them that some of them were probably easier on themselves than others and that this might affect their scores as well.

Tell them they will be put with partners and that whatever they say to each other should be held in confidence. During their discussions, participants may share their scores if they want to, but the emphasis should be on individual answers for which they scored lower than they wish they had.

# Action Plan

· · · · · · · · · · · ·

AFTER ADMINISTERING and debriefing the DAP, have participants partner up to discuss their findings. Partners can either be someone they know well who can give more insight into their behaviors or someone they don't know who could offer fresh insights.

Have pairs share where they landed on the Diversity Awareness Spectrum™ and discuss how that makes them feel (i.e., surprised, unnerved, or reassured). Have individuals take turns reflecting on the areas in which they scored high or low and prompt them to help each other brainstorm ways in which they can become stronger Change Agents at work.

After participants have debriefed the assessment, let them know that in order to add real value to their experience they need to apply what they have learned to their work environment. Display the Action Plan overhead and ask individuals to turn to the last page of the assessment and fill out the following:

- One thing you can start doing in the workplace
- One thing you can stop doing in the workplace
- One thing you can do differently starting today

Give participants time to complete their action plans and encourage them to share their ideas as a group.

# Powerpoint® Text

· · · · · · · · · · · · · · · · ·

AN ONLINE PRESENTATION of these slides
is available at www.pfeiffer.com/go/dap.

# Objectives

- Reflect on your day-to-day behaviors in the workplace.

- Get insights into the impact of your day-to-day behaviors.

- Learn how you can improve your behaviors to be more effective in your job and organization.

- Create an action plan.

# Instructions

- Read each statement and circle the number that best fits your behavior.

- Remember that there are no right or wrong answers.

- Be as honest and candid as possible with your responses.

- Consider each statement in terms of your personal values, beliefs, actions and reactions, and experiences.

- When you are finished, total the numbers you circled and write that total at the bottom of the page.

# Diversity Awareness Spectrum™

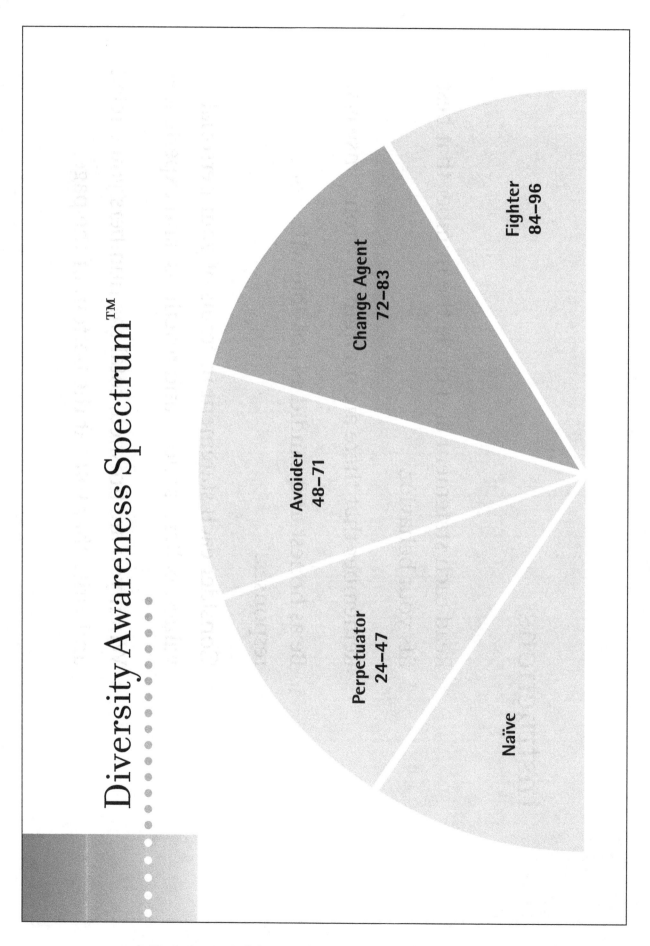

Fighter
84–96

Change Agent
72–83

Avoider
48–71

Perpetuator
24–47

Naïve

# Debriefing

| Naïve | Perpetuator | Avoider | Change Agent | Fighter |
|---|---|---|---|---|
| Acts with no knowledge or awareness of biases and prejudices and their negative impact. | Aware of biases and prejudices, but continues negative behaviors and reinforces stereotypes. | Tolerates unjust behavior in others and plays it safe. | Acts as a role model, takes action when appropriate, and addresses others' behaviors when necessary. | Always on the lookout for prejudice and sees it everywhere. |
| *"Clueless"* | *"Silent Troublemaker"* | *"Supporter"* | *"Risk Taker"* | *"Injustice Collector"* |

# Action Plan

- One thing you can start doing in the workplace

- One thing you can stop doing in the workplace

- One thing you can do differently starting today

# About the Author

. . . . . . . . . . . . . . . . .

KAREN M. STINSON, founder and CEO, started ProGroup more than twenty years ago with a vision of leading a highly skilled, multicultural, multi-disciplined team to partner with clients in creating supportive, productive workplaces. Today, her vision has become a living laboratory of more than one hundred diverse professionals committed to *creating inclusive cultures that work*, a concept proven over time to *Make Differences a Business Advantage™*. Strategic alliances with other organizations add even greater depth and expertise to ProGroup's offerings. If you have a need, ProGroup and its worldwide partners can meet it. She can be contacted at Karen@KarenStinson.com.

Karen is nationally known for her expertise in developing consultants who work with clients to create and facilitate long-range plans for organizational and professional growth. She has designed, tailored, and presented thousands of developmental programs and seminars for major organizations, many of which have been clients for nearly twenty years. Karen has received many awards, including the Trainer of Trainers Award from the American Society for Training and Development (ASTD) and the 2004 Changemaker Award from *The Business Journal*. She has been featured in numerous newspaper articles and has appeared on a variety of TV and radio shows.

Karen has consulted with individuals and organizations on various issues involving change in the workplace and marketplace. She and her team have worked with hundreds of major organizations to assess where they are, where they want to be, and how to get there. Recognized as one of the top diversity experts in the country, ProGroup has created and partnered in implementing and measuring thousands of strategic diversity initiatives.

Karen has developed several assessment instruments that are used globally and, together with her business partner, Myrna Marofsky, has created numerous award-winning videos, books, products, and e-learning tools currently available to clients.

Before founding ProGroup, Karen graduated from the University of Minnesota with degrees in education and business. She is also a published writer and has worked as a newspaper reporter, electrician, and welder. This unique blend of research skills, writing expertise, sales background, and employment experience, combined with experience gained in leading a multi-million-dollar consulting business, allows Karen to see eye -to-eye with a wide variety of people and organizations. She has a straightforward and entertaining style as a coach, speaker, trainer, and consultant. You can be assured that when you speak with Karen, she is telling you the truth.

# Pfeiffer Publications Guide

This guide is designed to familiarize you with the various types of Pfeiffer publications. The formats section describes the various types of products that we publish; the methodologies section describes the many different ways that content might be provided within a product. We also provide a list of the topic areas in which we publish.

## FORMATS

In addition to its extensive book-publishing program, Pfeiffer offers content in an array of formats, from fieldbooks for the practitioner to complete, ready-to-use training packages that support group learning.

**FIELDBOOK** Designed to provide information and guidance to practitioners in the midst of action. Most fieldbooks are companions to another, sometimes earlier, work, from which its ideas are derived; the fieldbook makes practical what was theoretical in the original text. Fieldbooks can certainly be read from cover to cover. More likely, though, you'll find yourself bouncing around following a particular theme, or dipping in as the mood, and the situation, dictate.

**HANDBOOK** A contributed volume of work on a single topic, comprising an eclectic mix of ideas, case studies, and best practices sourced by practitioners and experts in the field.

An editor or team of editors usually is appointed to seek out contributors and to evaluate content for relevance to the topic. Think of a handbook not as a ready-to-eat meal, but as a cookbook of ingredients that enables you to create the most fitting experience for the occasion.

**RESOURCE** Materials designed to support group learning. They come in many forms: a complete, ready-to-use exercise (such as a game); a comprehensive resource on one topic (such as conflict management) containing a variety of methods and approaches; or a collection of like-minded activities (such as icebreakers) on multiple subjects and situations.

**TRAINING PACKAGE** An entire, ready-to-use learning program that focuses on a particular topic or skill. All packages comprise a guide for the facilitator/trainer and a workbook for the participants. Some packages are supported with additional media—such as video—or learning aids, instruments, or other devices to help participants understand concepts or practice and develop skills.

- *Facilitator/trainer's guide* Contains an introduction to the program, advice on how to organize and facilitate the learning event, and step-by-step instructor notes. The guide also contains copies of presentation materials—handouts, presentations, and overhead designs, for example—used in the program.

- *Participant's workbook* Contains exercises and reading materials that support the learning goal and serves as a valuable reference and support guide for participants in the weeks and months that follow the learning event. Typically, each participant will require his or her own workbook.

**ELECTRONIC** CD-ROMs and web-based products transform static Pfeiffer content into dynamic, interactive experiences. Designed to take advantage of the searchability, automation, and ease-of-use that technology provides, our e-products bring convenience and immediate accessibility to your workspace.

# METHODOLOGIES

**CASE STUDY** A presentation, in narrative form, of an actual event that has occurred inside an organization. Case studies are not prescriptive, nor are they used to prove a point; they are designed to develop critical analysis and decision-making skills. A case study has a specific time frame, specifies a sequence of events, is narrative in structure, and contains a plot structure—an issue (what should be/have been done?). Use case studies when the goal is to enable participants to apply previously learned theories to the circumstances in the case, decide what is pertinent, identify the real issues, decide what should have been done, and develop a plan of action.

**ENERGIZER** A short activity that develops readiness for the next session or learning event. Energizers are most commonly used after a break or lunch to stimulate or refocus the group. Many involve some form of physical activity, so they are a useful way to counter post-lunch lethargy. Other uses include transitioning from one topic to another, where "mental" distancing is important.

**EXPERIENTIAL LEARNING ACTIVITY (ELA)** A facilitator-led intervention that moves participants through the learning cycle from experience to application (also known as a Structured Experience). ELAs are carefully thought-out designs in which there is a definite learning purpose and intended outcome. Each step—everything that participants do during the activity—facilitates the accomplishment of the stated goal. Each ELA includes complete instructions for facilitating the intervention and a clear statement of goals, suggested group size and timing, materials required, an explanation of the process, and, where appropriate, possible variations to the activity. (For more detail on Experiential Learning Activities, see the Introduction to the *Reference Guide to Handbooks and Annuals*, 1999 edition, Pfeiffer, San Francisco.)

**GAME** A group activity that has the purpose of fostering team spirit and togetherness in addition to the achievement of a pre-stated goal. Usually contrived—undertaking a desert expedition, for example—this type of learning method offers an engaging means for participants to demonstrate and practice business and interpersonal skills. Games are effective for team building and personal development mainly because the goal is subordinate to the process—the means through which participants reach decisions, collaborate, communicate, and generate trust and understanding. Games often engage teams in "friendly" competition.

**ICEBREAKER** A (usually) short activity designed to help participants overcome initial anxiety in a training session and/or to acquaint the participants with one another. An icebreaker can be a fun activity or can be tied to specific topics or training goals. While a useful tool in itself, the icebreaker comes into its own in situations where tension or resistance exists within a group.

**INSTRUMENT** A device used to assess, appraise, evaluate, describe, classify, and summarize various aspects of human behavior. The term used to describe an instrument depends primarily on its format and purpose. These terms include survey, questionnaire, inventory, diagnostic, survey, and poll. Some uses of instruments include providing instrumental feedback to group members, studying here-and-now processes or functioning within a group, manipulating group composition, and evaluating outcomes of training and other interventions.

Instruments are popular in the training and HR field because, in general, more growth can occur if an individual is provided with a method for focusing specifically on his or her own behavior. Instruments also are used to obtain information that will serve as a basis for change and to assist in workforce planning efforts.

Paper-and-pencil tests still dominate the instrument landscape with a typical package comprising a facilitator's guide, which offers advice on administering the instrument and interpreting the collected data, and an initial set of instruments. Additional instruments are available separately. Pfeiffer, though, is investing heavily in e-instruments. Electronic instrumentation provides effortless distribution and, for larger groups particularly, offers advantages over paper-and-pencil tests in the time it takes to analyze data and provide feedback.

**LECTURETTE** A short talk that provides an explanation of a principle, model, or process that is pertinent to the participants' current learning needs. A lecturette is intended to establish a common language bond between the trainer and the participants by providing a mutual frame of reference. Use a lecturette as an introduction to a group activity or event, as an interjection during an event, or as a handout.

**MODEL** A graphic depiction of a system or process and the relationship among its elements. Models provide a frame of reference and something more tangible, and more easily remembered, than a verbal explanation. They also give participants something to "go on," enabling them to track their own progress as they experience the dynamics, processes, and relationships being depicted in the model.

**ROLE PLAY** A technique in which people assume a role in a situation/scenario: a customer service rep in an angry-customer exchange, for example. The way in which the role is approached is then discussed and feedback is offered. The role play is often repeated using a different approach and/or incorporating changes made based on feedback received. In other words, role playing is a spontaneous interaction involving realistic behavior under artificial (and safe) conditions.

**SIMULATION** A methodology for understanding the interrelationships among components of a system or process. Simulations differ from games in that they test or use a model that depicts or mirrors some aspect of reality in form, if not necessarily in content. Learning occurs by studying the effects of change on one or more factors of the model. Simulations are commonly used to test hypotheses about what happens in a system—often referred to as "what if?" analysis—or to examine best-case/worst-case scenarios.

**THEORY** A presentation of an idea from a conjectural perspective. Theories are useful because they encourage us to examine behavior and phenomena through a different lens.

## TOPICS

The twin goals of providing effective and practical solutions for workforce training and organization development and meeting the educational needs of training and human resource professionals shape Pfeiffer's publishing program. Core topics include the following:

Leadership & Management
Communication & Presentation
Coaching & Mentoring
Training & Development
E-Learning
Teams & Collaboration
OD & Strategic Planning
Human Resources
Consulting

# What will you find on pfeiffer.com?

- The best in workplace performance solutions for training and HR professionals

- Downloadable training tools, exercises, and content

- Web-exclusive offers

- Training tips, articles, and news

- Seamless on-line ordering

- Author guidelines, information on becoming a Pfeiffer Affiliate, and much more

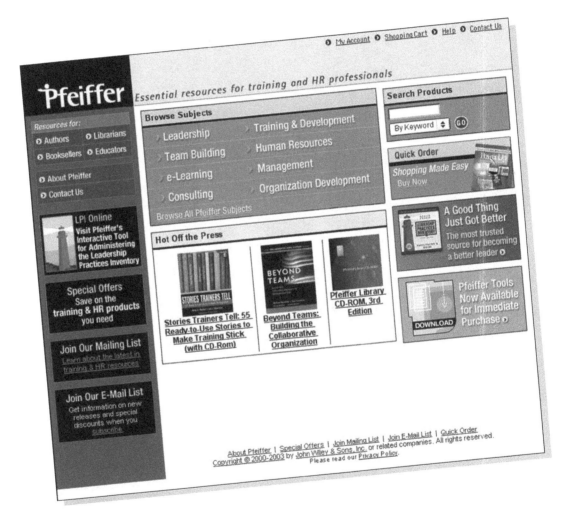